# PAINTED
# POTS

# PAINTED
# POTS

*Over 20 inspirational projects for
the home and garden*

Consultant editor: Simona Hill

LORENZ BOOKS

First published in 2000 by
Lorenz Books

© Anness Publishing Limited 2000

Lorenz Books
is an imprint of
Anness Publishing Limited
Hermes House
88–89 Blackfriars Road
London SE1 8HA

This edition distributed in Canada by Raincoast Books,
8680 Cambie Street, Vancouver, British Columbia V6P 6M9

Published in the USA by Lorenz Books,
Anness Publishing Inc., 27 West 20th Street,
New York, NY 10011; (800) 354-9657

ISBN 0 7548 0460 7

A CIP catalogue record for this book is available from the British Library

Publisher: Joanna Lorenz
Project Editor: Simona Hill
Designer: Simon Wilder
Editorial Reader: Hayley Kerr
Production Controller: Claire Rae

Printed and bound in Singapore

1 3 5 7 9 10 8 6 4 2

# Contents

# Introduction

* *Give new terracotta pots character with simple painted designs in bold, bright colours.*

From the earliest times, people all over the world have fashioned vessels from clay, glass and metal. The process of manufacture which they used helped to define the nature of their civilizations. In almost every case, they were more than simple containers: every culture decorated its creations in some way, marking them with the identity of the society or the maker of the pot.

Surface decoration on pots can take the form of either texture or colour, or a combination of the two. Since clay is a malleable substance – that is, it can be moulded with the hands – the most basic form of ornament is the impression of the potter's fingers. The soft clay can be incised, engraved, stamped or indented to produce detailed patterns in low relief. Conversely, applied decoration involves adding extra pieces of clay to the surface to build up a three-dimensional pattern. Modern, mass-produced ceramics, from dinner services to flower pots, can be decorated with moulded motifs, and if you have never tried painting ceramics before, excellent effects are easy to achieve by simply colouring the raised pottery decorations.

Coloured decoration can be introduced using slip – clay mixed with water to give a creamy consistency. This may be made from

clay that is naturally a different colour to that used for the body of the pot, or it may be stained using a metal oxide such as copper or cobalt.

Once made, the pot is traditionally glazed. The fundamental purpose of a glaze is to render the porous clay watertight and give it a smooth surface, but its decorative function has always been just as important. Ancient Egyptian potters probably developed the earliest glazed ceramic surface, known as faience or Egyptian paste, usually in a rich turquoise colour produced using copper oxide. The glaze is fused to the clay during firing, creating a hard, glassy finish.

✳ *Decorate plain white vases with designs that complement your interior colour scheme.*

Painted decorations can be applied to unglazed pots before or after firing, or to unfired glaze. In all these cases, the porous surface means that each brush stroke is irrevocable, calling for sureness of touch on the part of the painter. The brush needs to be handled freely to develop a fluid line. In the subsequent firing, the decoration becomes an integral part of the ceramic, with the brush strokes accentuated and the colour modified by the glaze. Enamels applied on top of the fired glaze cannot achieve the same degree of permanence and are not so hard-wearing, even when high-fired, though they do retain their brilliant colours and sharp definition.

More delicate still are decorations which are not fired at all, though their impermanence may actually contribute to their charm. If you are using such techniques on your own pots, a judicious amount of distressing can give an attractive appearance of age. Gilding is simply glued on to both pottery and glass.

✳ *Strategically-placed old garden equipment makes a pleasing visual display.*

* *Gilding is a deceptively simple technique that will give your pots an elegant finish.*

Ordinary house paints can be used to decorate terracotta pots for the garden: the colour will fade fairly quickly, but probably not before you have planned a new colour scheme anyway.

An even more ephemeral treatment for garden pots consists of painting designs using liquid seaweed plant food, which will encourage the growth of algae and give the appearance of age. Undiluted, the colour is a very deep brown and looks beautiful decorating terracotta. You can preserve this rich colour with a coat of varnish or leave the pots unsealed: most of the coating will wear away, leaving soft faded patterns like traces of ancient frescoes.

The evolution of pottery has an 8,000 year history, yet the materials and many of the techniques used have remained almost constant, so that some of the world's oldest pots look as familiar and serviceable today as the work of modern potters. A huge legacy of ethnic and historic decorative styles is freely available to us today, and continues to influence modern ceramic design. With the development of water-based enamel paints which do not need to be fired at high temperatures in a kiln, but can be hardened in a domestic oven, anyone can try their hand at decorating pots at home. Though you may not be able to use ceramic techniques, there is no reason why you should not imitate the decorative effects produced by potters with glazes and slips: try spattering, pouring, etching and sponging, as well as painting with a brush.

* *Simple designs work well on glass.*

Everyone uses pots all the time – it would be impossible to manage without them. You eat and drink from bowls, cups and glasses, store food in jars, use pots both indoors and outdoors to hold plants and flowers. So decorated pots can be more than just ornaments: you can use your creations every day. Whether you choose to imitate traditional patterns, or decorate modern pieces in completely original ways, you can produce painted pots that are both beautiful and functional.

*Painted Pots* presents a whole array of imaginative and easily achievable methods of decorating your pots, whether they are brand new pieces of white china, or weathered old containers in need of a facelift. There are so many exciting paint ranges available for glass, china, metal and wood, that almost any surface can be given some decorative treatment.

The advantage of designing and painting your own china is the thrill of creating something beautiful and unique. Almost any shape of item can be painted with the design of your choice to suit the internal decor of your home. Garden planters and containers can be decorated to show off favourite blooms to best effect in the garden, and as your display changes, so too can the colour of the pots. Start with simple paint washes, or geometric designs, then move on to freehand designs. The creative pleasure of painting doesn't stop when you put your paints away – you can enjoy living with your decorations for years to come.

❋ *Stamping is a quick and easy method of applying colour to china. Use a purchased stamp or design your own.*

❋ *Flat surfaces are the easiest on which to paint and a good opportunity to try out more complex designs.*

# *Indoor Pots*

Whether they hold flowers in the living room or pasta in the kitchen, jars, vases and pots can be both useful and decorative in every room. You probably already have several pots that can be given a new lease of life by adding pretty painted motifs. Even cracked ones can be painted as long as you want to use them solely for decoration. If you are buying new pieces to paint, plain white china is often cheaper than anything with a coloured glaze or elaborate decoration, and is the most versatile for painting.

Before embarking on a new project, test the brushes and colours you are using on an unwanted piece of china. White ceramic tiles are ideal, and are also useful as palettes for mixing paint. Water-based enamel paints can be hardened in a domestic oven, which will make them durable and dishwasher-proof, while solvent-based paints are for decorative use only, and must not come into contact with food.

Metallic effects look exciting and opulent, and you can gild both pottery and glass, combining it if you wish with other decorative effects. Ordinary terracotta pots, gilded and filled with candle wax, make beautiful, sparkling lights for a festive tablecentre.

# ❋ *Citrus Fruit Bowl* ❋

*The perfect decoration for a fruit bowl, these zingy limes are painted using a combination of stencilling and freehand painting to give an ordered but excitingly spontaneous result.*

## You will need

soft pencil

tracing paper

stencil sheet

craft knife

cutting mat

masking tape

plain ceramic bowl

yellow chinagraph pencil (china marker)

paintbrushes

acrylic enamel paints in citrus green, medium green, dark green and yellow

palette

acrylic varnish (optional)

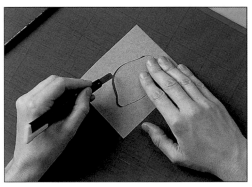

1 Draw a lime freehand on tracing paper using a soft pencil and transfer the shape to a stencil sheet. Cut out using a craft knife.

2 Attach the stencil to the bowl using masking tape. Draw inside the stencil using a yellow chinagraph pencil (china marker). Repeat all over the bowl.

3 Paint the limes in citrus green. Let the paint dry, then add medium green highlights. Paint a dark green stalk at the end of each lime.

4 Paint the background yellow, leaving a thin outline around each lime. Varnish the bowl, or bake to harden the paint, following the manufacturer's instructions.

# ❋ Kitchen Herb Jars ❋

*Dried herbs deteriorate quickly in the light, so are best stored in china.
A set of small plain jars can be prettily decorated and, if you wish, you
can include the name of each herb in the central panel of this design.*

## You will need

soft pencil

tracing paper

carbon paper

masking tape

plain ceramic herb jars

blue chinagraph pencil (china marker)

acrylic enamel paints in blue, lime green, dark green and turquoise

palette

paintbrushes

dried-out felt-tipped pen

1 Copy one large and one small leaf design on to tracing paper. Attach the tracings to carbon paper, ink side down, using masking tape.

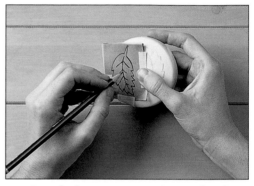

2 Attach the tracings to a jar and redraw the outlines to transfer the design. Use the large leaf on the lid and the small leaf all over the jar. Leave a space on one side.

3 With a blue chinagraph (china marker), draw an oval in the space and fill with blue. Before it dries, write in the panel using a felt-tipped pen, to remove paint.

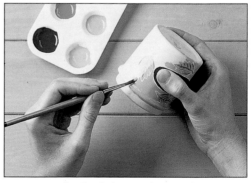

4 Paint the herb leaves lime. Allow to dry. Add the veins in dark green and dry. Paint the background turquoise, leaving a thin outline around each image.

# ❋ Simple Spongeware ❋

*The simple folk-art motifs and gentle colouring of traditional spongeware are easy to recreate using enamel paint. This paint is for decorative use only.*

## You will need

tracing paper

pencil

spray adhesive

stencil sheet

craft knife

cutting mat

scissors

plain white ceramic jug (pitcher)

acrylic enamel paints in brown, yellow-orange, yellow, blue and green

palette

small natural sponge

1 Trace the cat template, then cut out a hexagon larger than the cat. Stick each to a stencil sheet and cut out. Attach the cat stencil to the side of the jug (pitcher).

2 Mix a deep orange using brown and yellow-orange paint, and apply through the stencil using a sponge. Leave to dry, then peel off the stencil.

3 Adhere the back of the hexagon and stick over the cat. Sponge green paint over the whole jug. Apply paint densely around the hexagon and the rim.

4 Peel off the paper and bake the jug to harden the paint, following the manufacturer's instructions.

# ✳ *Marine Painted Carafe* ✳

*Add an extra dimension to plain glassware with simple seashore motifs.*
*Keep to natural objects, like pieces of seaweed, shells and starfish, and*
*scatter them sparingly over the glass using opaque white glass paint.*

## You will need

glass carafe

lint-free cotton cloth

methylated spirits
(turpentine)

tracing paper

pencil

scissors

masking tape

carbon paper

paintbrush

white glass paint

1 Wipe the surface of the glass with a lint-free cloth dipped in methylated spirits (turpentine) to ensure that the surface is grease-free.

2 Trace the templates at the back of the book, or draw your own designs freehand on a sheet of tracing paper.

3 Cut round the motifs and stick them on to the carafe, placing a piece of carbon paper under each one, ink side down. Redraw over the outlines.

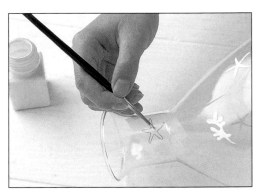

4 Using a fine paintbrush, paint the outines, and fill in the shapes with white glass paint.

# ✽ Gilded Amphora ✽

*This new amphora has been given the look of an ancestral treasure, using gilding and a lapis lazuli paint effect. A dotting of amber shellac enhances the illusion of age.*

## You will need

terracotta amphora

pale blue spray paint

acrylic paints in ultramarine, black, white, yellow ochre and viridian green

texture gel

palettes

large stencil brush

pencil (optional)

water-based size

paintbrushes

gold Dutch metal leaf

soft cloth

water-based varnishing wax

amber shellac

old stiff-bristled brush

water spray

old sheet or towel

matt acrylic varnish

1 Wash and dry the amphora. Spray with an even coat of pale blue paint. Leave to dry. Mix some ultramarine acrylic paint with texture gel.

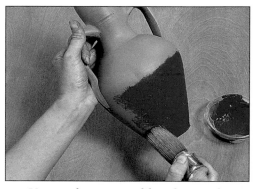

2 Using a large stencil brush, stipple a heavy coat around the lower half of the pot (draw a guideline around the middle if necessary). Leave until dry and hard.

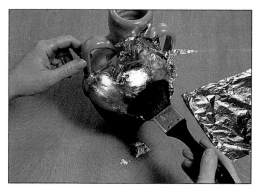

3 Paint water-based size on the top half of the amphora. Leave until tacky. Gild the sized area with metal leaf. Using a soft cloth, burnish the gilding.

4 Paint varnishing wax on to the surface. Leave to dry, then buff with a soft cloth. Dab shellac on to the gilded surface to look like rust. Leave to dry.

*Continued over* ➤

5 Thin some black acrylic paint with water and paint random areas of the lower half of the pot, keeping the strokes diagonal. Leave to dry.

6 Mix ultramarine paint with a little white and thin with water. Paint some other random areas of the lower half of the pot with this. Leave to dry.

7 Thin yellow ochre, white and black acrylic paint with water in three separate containers. Load an old, stiff-bristled brush with one colour at a time and flick a fine spray of paint over the surface of the pot.

8 Mix a verdigris colour using two parts viridian green to one part white, and thin with water. Place the pot on an old sheet or towel. Apply some paint to the top half of the pot and disperse with the water spray so that the colour dribbles down. When the paint is dry, give the whole pot a thin, even coat of matt acrylic varnish.

# ✳ Sunflower Vase ✳

*Sunflowers are a perennially popular motif as their bold shapes and warm, cheerful colours represent the essence of summer. On this striking vase, they stand out against a background of deep sky-blue.*

## You will need

tracing paper

soft pencil

white ceramic vase

masking tape

yellow and blue chinagraph pencils (china markers)

acrylic enamel paints in yellow, pale green, light brown, dark green, very light brown and sky-blue

palette

medium and fine paintbrushes

1 Draw the sunflower freehand on a sheet of tracing paper. Turn the tracing over and stick it to the side of the vase. Rub over the tracing to transfer the image.

2 Repeat all over the vase. Carefully highlight each design with a yellow chinagraph pencil (china marker).

3 Fill in the sunflower petals with yellow and the stalks and leaves of the design with pale green paint. Put the vase on one side and leave to dry.

4 Paint the flower centres light brown, adding a ring of short lines around the edge of each. Add some dabs of very light brown to each flower centre. Leave to dry.

*Continued over* ➤

5 Paint the leaf veins using a darker shade of green. Leave to dry.

6 Fill in the background using sky-blue enamel paint, leaving a narrow white outline around each flower. Leave to dry.

7 Finally, draw around the outline and centre details of each flower using a blue chinagraph pencil (china marker).

# ❋ *Vegetable Storage Jars* ❋

*Storage jars are always useful, either for you to use or to give as presents, and when adorned with bold designs like these colourful vegetables, they look great on kitchen shelves.*

## You will need

tracing paper

soft pencil

plain paper

spray adhesive

carbon paper

craft knife or scissors

plain ceramic storage jars

clear adhesive tape

felt-tipped pen

acrylic enamel paints in turquoise, coral, ivory, blue and yellow

paintbrushes

palette

1 Trace the templates and transfer the designs to plain paper. Adhere the paper to a sheet of carbon paper, ink side down. Cut roughly around each design.

2 Tape some of the designs on to one of the jars. Redraw the outlines to transfer the designs. Remove the paper and repeat on the other jars and lids.

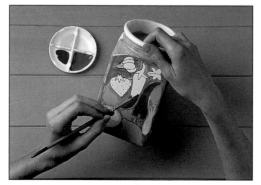

3 Paint the background turquoise. Leave to dry. Mix red using coral and ivory and paint the chillis (chiles). Mix blue and yellow for the leaves. Leave to dry.

4 Add the details to the vegetables in blue. Paint the rims yellow and add small ivory dots all over the background. When dry, bake to harden the paints.

# ❋ Stamped Grapes ❋

*Ready-made stamps can be used to decorate plain ceramics in minutes using acrylic enamel paint. If you are using a combination of stamps, it's a good idea to test the motifs on paper.*

## You will need

white ceramic jug (pitcher)

clean cloth

grape, tendril and leaf stamps

black stamp pad

scrap paper

scissors

acrylic enamel paints in black and ultramarine

old plate

foam roller

1 Wash the jug (pitcher) in hot water and detergent and wipe dry to ensure that the surface is free of grease.

2 Print a bunch of grapes, a tendril and a leaf on scrap paper and cut them out. Arrange them on the jug to plan the shape of your design.

3 Mix the black and blue enamel paints together on a flat plate. Run the roller through the paint until it is evenly coated, ink the stamps and stamp the design.

4 If necessary, use the leaf again to fill the design. Bake to harden the paint, following the manufacturer's instructions.

# ✳ Gilded Glass Vase ✳

*Frosted glass is especially suitable for gilding as its slightly rough surface provides the perfect key for size. Use this technique only for decorative pieces — it is not a good idea to gild glasses you will use.*

## You will need

water-based size

paintbrush

frosted glass vase

Dutch metal leaf in copper and silver

soft cloth

pencil

stencil sheet

craft knife

cutting mat

stencil brush

water-based varnishing wax

1 Paint a thin coat of water-based size around the rim and foot of the vase and leave for 20–30 minutes, until it becomes tacky.

2 Gild the sized areas with copper Dutch metal leaf. Burnish gently with a soft cloth to remove the excess leaf.

3 Trace the template and transfer it to a stencil sheet. Cut out the design. Stipple size through the stencil, all around the vase. Leave to become tacky.

4 Gild the motifs with silver Dutch metal leaf, burnish, and seal the gilded areas with water-based varnishing wax. Polish with a soft cloth.

# ❋ Terracotta Laundry Pot ❋

*Putting laundry in a flower pot sounds unusual, but it makes a refreshing change from a wicker basket. Terracotta pots are available in all sizes and this technique will give a pristine pot an antique feel.*

## You will need

rag

shellac

large terracotta flower pot

white emulsion (latex) paint

paintbrushes

scouring pad

sandpaper (optional)

1 Soak a rag in shellac and rub the surface of the pot with it. The polish will sink in very quickly, leaving a yellow sheen on the surface.

2 Dilute the emulsion (latex) paint with an equal amount of water. Stir it well and apply a coat to the pot. Leave to dry.

3 Rub the pot with the scouring pad to remove most of the white paint. The paint will cling to the crevices and mouldings to resemble limescale. If you wish, rub it back further using sandpaper.

4 When you are happy with the effect, apply a coat of shellac with a brush to seal the surface.

# Outdoor Pots

Out in the garden, the most flexible colour can be added with pots and containers. By planting up moveable pots you can put the colour where you want it, and re-plant with new seasonal colour as the old blooms die down. As well as their contents, the pots themselves can be decorated to add colour and style. Inexpensive, machine-made terracotta pots can be made distinctive using simple stencilled designs. Choose paint colours that will enhance your plants and look good within your garden's colour scheme. Terracotta is porous and will absorb a lot of paint, so you may need several coats. You can start with an undercoat to seal the porous surface, but if you do without you will achieve an uneven finish which works well with the rough feel of terracotta. Solvent-based paints will weather and fade if the pots are placed outdoors, but this will add to their charm.

Your choice does not have to be restricted to garden pots. Many other containers can be filled with plants, as long as drainage holes can be drilled in the base. Try using old chimney pots, buckets, or traditional wooden trugs. Match wooden boxes to your plants season by season, ringing the changes with a lick of paint to maximize the impact of your chosen colour scheme.

# ❋ *Terracotta Pots* ❋

*The sunny yellow and green of spring daffodils served as the inspiration
for the colour-scheme used for this group of pots. In summer, they
could be filled with yellow pansies, marigolds or nasturtiums.*

## *You will need*

terracotta flower
pots with deep rims

soft pencil

tape measure

solvent-based or
acrylic enamel paint
in green, lime green
and yellow

paintbrushes

palette

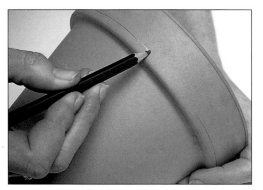

**1** Draw parallel lines around the top and bottom of the flower pot rim. Measure the circumference of the rim and divide it into equal sections. Mark with a pencil.

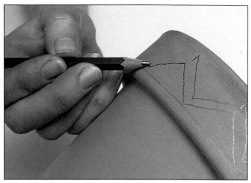

**2** Draw a double zigzag line around the rim, joining the pencil marks, and paint the triangles green. Leave the rest of the rim unpainted.

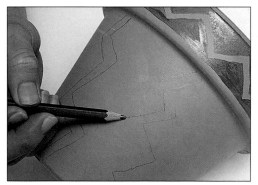

**3** Draw vertical zigzags down the body of the pot under each alternate zigzag on the rim. Paint these lime green.

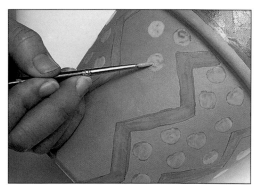

**4** Randomly dot the area between the zigzags with yellow, and leave to dry. If you are using acrylic paint, bake the pots to harden the paint.

# *Strawberry Fruit Basket*

*This decorative planter would look lovely filled with herbs on
a kitchen windowsill, or, of course, with
strawberry plants.*

## You will need

sandpaper

wooden planter

paintbrushes

white emulsion
(latex) paint

tracing paper

pencil

scissors

medium-density
sponge, such as a
kitchen sponge

marker pen

craft knife

cutting mat

acrylic paints in red,
green and yellow

palette

clear acrylic varnish

1 Lightly sand the planter and paint it white. Draw a strawberry and leaf freehand. Draw around them on the sponge and cut out using a craft knife.

2 Load the strawberry stamp with paint and stamp on the planter. Allow to dry. Stamp the calyces in green. Make the large leaves by stamping three times.

3 Allow the leaves to dry, then use a pencil to mark the positions of the stems and paint them freehand using a fine paintbrush.

4 Use a fine paintbrush to paint yellow pips on the strawberries. Leave to dry, then apply at least two coats of acrylic varnish.

# ❈ Marbled Pots ❈

*These pots have been marbled in random, swirling patterns. The
technique will work on terracotta, but for a more dramatic effect, paint
the pots first with two base coats of emulsion (latex) paint.*

## You will need

painted terracotta
pot

wire

plastic washing-up
bowl (dishpan)

gloss paint

1 Run a length of wire through the hole
in the pot base and twist the wire ends
to make a loop. Fill a bowl (dishpan) with
water and drizzle paint on to the surface.

2 Swirl the paint into a pattern on the
surface then, using the wire handle,
lower the pot into the water so that gloss
paint adheres to one side.

3 Turn the pot over carefully and dip
the other side into the water.

4 Hang up the pot, still on its wire
handle, and leave to dry for 24 hours.

# ✳ *Tiled Window Box* ✳

*These bright painted tiles were inspired by the decorated exterior tiles
seen in Portugal. They have been used to cover the front and sides of a
ready-made wooden window box.*

## You will need

tracing paper

pencil

15cm/6in square
white tiles

15 x 7.5cm/6 x 3in
white edging tiles

carbon paper

masking tape

masking paper

craft knife

cutting mat

paintbrushes

masking fluid

acrylic enamel paint
in bright yellow and
dark blue

polyurethane
varnish

**1** Enlarge and trace the template to suit your tiles. Match the design across the tiles. Tape the tracing down with a sheet of carbon paper, ink side down, below. Redraw the design to transfer it to the tiles.

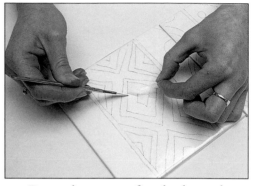

**2** Down the centre of each tile, stick a rectangle of masking paper wide enough to cover the central blue stripe and the white stripes. Cut out and remove the paper from all the blue areas.

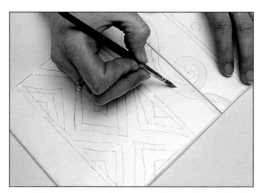

**3** Using a paintbrush and masking fluid, thickly paint in the scroll, working over two tiles at a time. Leave to dry.

**4** Carefully paint the blue and yellow stripes aiming for a flat, even coat. Leave to dry.

5 Run a blade along the edges of the paper to free the paint. Cut along both sides of the masking fluid and peel it off.

6 Outline the white scroll in blue and paint yellow centres in the diamonds. When dry, bake the tiles to harden them. Apply several coats of varnish.

# ❋ *Verdigris Bucket* ❋

*There is something irresistible about the luminous, blue-green tones of verdigris. It is a colour that always complements plants and it is not difficult to reproduce.*

## You will need

galvanized buckets

medium-grade sandpaper

metal primer

paintbrushes

acrylic paints in gold, white, aqua and rust

amber shellac

natural sponge

polyurethane varnish

**1** Sand the buckets, then prime with metal primer and allow to dry. Give each bucket a coat of gold acrylic paint and leave to dry.

**2** Add a coat of shellac. Allow to dry. For verdigris, mix white and aqua paint and dilute to a watery consistency. For the rust, mix white with rust and dilute.

❋ *Plaster copies of statues are a sympathetic base for verdigris paint-effects.*

**3** Sponge the thinned paint over the shellac, allowing the gold base coat to show through in places, and leave to dry before applying a coat of varnish.

# ❋ *Lead Chimney* ❋

*Lead has been used to make containers for centuries, but it is very
expensive, so here is a way of imitating it, using a plastic chimney and
a simple paint effect.*

## You will need

sandpaper

plastic, terracotta-
coloured chimney

acrylic primer

paintbrushes

emulsion (latex)
paint in charcoal-
grey and white

acrylic scumble
glaze

polyurethane
varnish

**1** Sand the chimney to give a key for the paint. Paint with a coat of acrylic primer and leave to dry.

**2** Apply a coat of charcoal-grey emulsion (latex) paint over the entire surface and leave to dry.

**3** Tint some scumble glaze with white emulsion and thin with water. Paint over the chimney randomly. Blend the colour by washing over the surface with a wet brush and leave to dry.

**4** Add more of the white scumble mixture to parts of the chimney in a random effect to "age" the surface. Leave to dry, then paint the whole chimney with a coat of polyurethane varnish.

# ❋ Spotted Flower Pots ❋

*Stamped terracotta pots will give a new, fresh look to your patio or windowsill. Light, bright colours suit this pattern really well, but you can make them as subtle or as bold as you please.*

## You will need

terracotta flower pots

white acrylic primer

paintbrushes

emulsion (latex) paint in yellow, white, red and blue

old plate

small foam rollers

satin acrylic varnish

**1** Make sure the flower pots are clean and dry. Prime them with a coat of white acrylic primer and leave to dry.

**2** Thin some yellow emulsion (latex) paint with water and colourwash the pot using a dry brush and random brush strokes. Allow to dry.

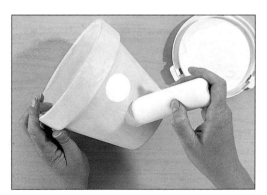

**3** Put some white paint in a palette. Press the end of a roller into the paint, then press it firmly on to the flower pot. Repeat all over the pot. Leave to dry.

**4** Repeat using red paint, positioning the roller slightly to one side of each white spot. Colour some of the spots blue. Leave to dry. Seal with varnish.

# ✻ Stencilled Bucket ✻

*Turn an ordinary household bucket into a stylish garden pot. This stencil is based on an old design found on the walls of a Rhode Island house. Repeat the flower design around the side of the bucket.*

## You will need

tracing paper

pencil

spray adhesive

stencil sheet

craft knife

cutting mat

spray paint in bright green and yellow

galvanized bucket

masking tape

scrap paper

**1** Trace the template and adhere it to a stencil sheet. Cut out the shapes with a craft knife and peel off the template. Make your own border template.

**2** In a well-ventilated area, spray the bucket green and leave to dry thoroughly. You may need to apply several coats to obtain an even covering.

**3** Spray the back of the flower stencil lightly with adhesive. Position the stencil on the bucket.

**4** Tape scrap paper around the stencil. Spray with yellow paint. Lift off when dry to the touch and re-position. Spray the border in the same way.

# Mexican Painted Pots

*Rings of folk-art motifs painted over stripes of vibrant colours give simple pots a rich Mexican look. Stacked together and planted up with pelargoniums in hot summer colours, they make a lively garden feature.*

## You will need

terracotta pots with fluted tops

masking tape

white acrylic primer

paintbrushes

gouache poster colours

polyurethane varnish

**1** Mark the stripes on each pot using different widths of masking tape. The areas covered with masking tape will remain natural terracotta.

**2** Paint the main body of the pot, below the rim, with white acrylic primer. Leave to dry thoroughly.

**3** Paint the coloured stripes, changing colour for each band. Leave to dry, then peel off the masking tape.

**4** Using a fine brush and the white primer, paint a series of traditional motifs along the stripes. When completely dry, coat with varnish.

# ❈ Mosaic Flower Pot and Saucer ❈

*Make a feature of an ordinary flower pot with a bright interior colour
and an exterior checkerboard design that looks like mosaic, but is
actually easy and quick to stamp on in brilliant enamel paints.*

## You will need

terracotta flower pot
and saucer

erasers

craft knife

solvent-based or
acrylic enamel
paints in dark blue,
green, yellow and
lilac

palette

scrap paper

paintbrushes

**1** Wash and dry the flower pot and saucer. Cut the erasers into long rectangular blocks, all the same size. Cut one for each colour.

**2** Test-print each colour on paper, then print two rows of squares around the rim of the pot in a random sequence of colours, leaving small gaps between each.

**3** Print around the main body of the pot, making the gaps between the squares narrower as you work down, to accommodate the tapering shape. Leave to dry.

**4** Paint the inside of the saucer. Do not paint the rim. Leave to dry. Paint the inside of the pot. If you are using acrylic paints, bake the pots to harden them.

# ✳ *Techniques* ✳

*The projects in this book do not require any specialist skills but it is worth practising a few painting techniques before you start. The tips and techniques suggested below will prove useful.*

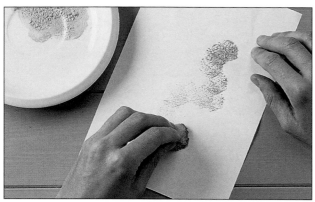

**TESTING A SPONGE** Load the sponge with paint, and test the print on paper. The first prints will be too saturated with paint to achieve a pleasing effect.

**PRINTING BLOCKS** When using printing blocks, roll the block lightly on to the surface to ensure you get a good even print. Test the print first.

**REMOVING MASKING TAPE OR FILM** Remove tape before the paint is completely dry as this will give a cleaner edge to the pattern beneath.

**USING PAINTBRUSHES** Use an appropriately-sized brush for the task in hand. Paint large areas with a large brush. A small, fine brush is best for details.

**TESTING NEW TECHNIQUES** Always test out a technique that you have not tried before. Apply the new technique to a spare piece of china, which can be cleaned up easily, rather than a piece you are already in the process of decorating.

**SPONGING VARIATIONS** A stencilled design can be made more interesting by varying the density of the sponging within the image or by adding more than one colour. Allowing the first coat of paint to dry partially before the application of the second will mean that there is more contrast and less blending of the two colours.

## PREPARING A STENCIL

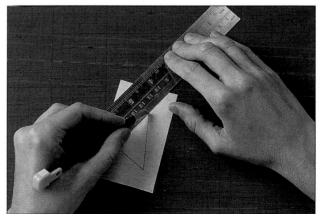

1 Draw a freehand shape or trace and transfer a template from the back of the book on to a piece of stencil card (cardboard).

2 Using a craft knife or scalpel, metal ruler and self-healing cutting mat, cut away the shape, leaving the stencil card border intact.

# ❋ Templates ❋

*Enlarge the templates on a photocopier to the desired size.*

Gilded Glass Vase

Marine Painted Carafe

Simple Spongeware

Tiled Window Box

Stencilled Bucket

Borage Pot

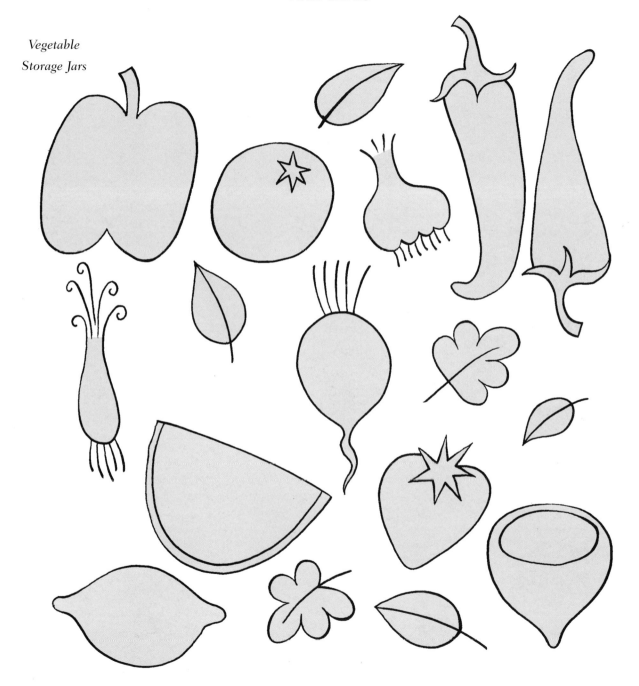

*Vegetable
Storage Jars*

# *   $\mathcal{I}ndex$   *

 $\mathcal{A}cknowledgements$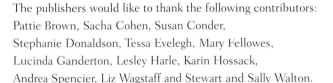

The publishers would like to thank the following contributors:
Pattie Brown, Sacha Cohen, Susan Conder,
Stephanie Donaldson, Tessa Evelegh, Mary Fellowes,
Lucinda Ganderton, Lesley Harle, Karin Hossack,
Andrea Spencier, Liz Wagstaff and Stewart and Sally Walton.

Thanks also to the following photographers:
Simon McBride, Rodney Forte, Michelle Garrett,
Lizzie Orme, Debbie Patterson, Graham Rae and Mark Wood,